ROOTED IN WONDER

Celebrating the World's National Trees

Written by Michelle Cusolito

Illustrated by Marya Wright

MOON BIRD

Trees—
the tallest,
heaviest,
and oldest
living things on Earth.

Wherever you live,
you can see a tree.

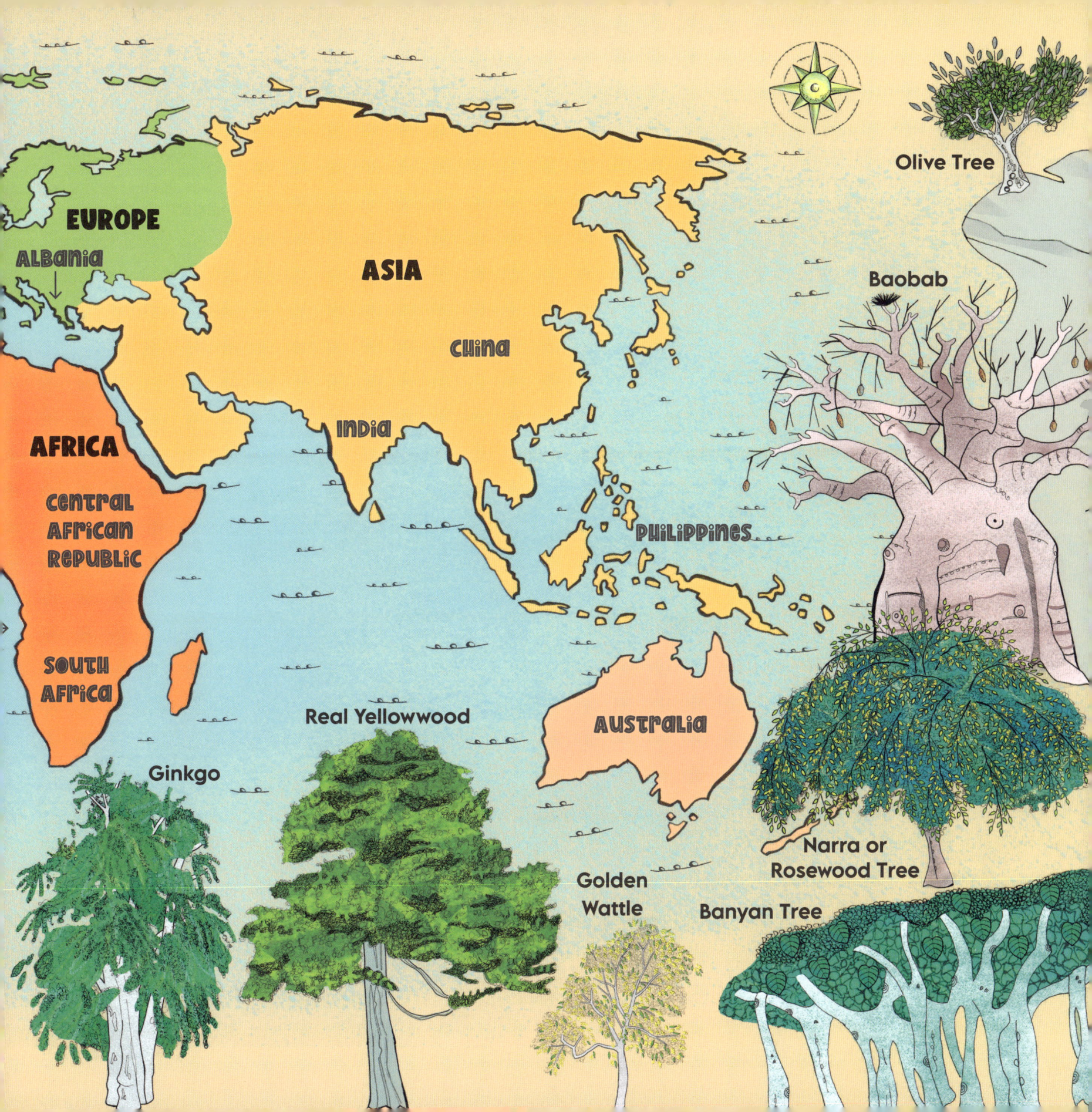

DEDICATION

Michelle:

To my niblings Luca, Zoe, Zeke and Evo, who started climbing the tree outside my window before they could reach the lowest branch.

Marya:

For my wonderful supportive husband and family. Special thanks to Fiona, Liz, Gemma and Richard.

They survive on the edges of dry, dusty deserts,

along busy city streets,

and in steamy green rainforests.

They perch on wind-swept seaside cliffs, cling to steep mountainsides,

and withstand howling winds in the Arctic tundra.

Trees
are symbols
of growth and stability,
strength and endurance.

Most countries have chosen a national
tree that represents their resources,
values, history, and culture.

There are many kinds of national trees,
like these ...

Banyan Tree
(Ficus benghalensis)
National Tree of India

Banyan seeds land in the crook of other trees, then sprout and send snake-like aerial roots down from the canopy to the ground.

The roots thicken
and become
wooden pillars,
making one tree
seem like a whole forest.

Children play
in their branches.
Adults shelter
in the shade of the canopy,
to converse and confide,
barter and bargain.

Golden Wattle

(Acacia pycnantha)

National Tree of Australia

Shrub-like golden wattles
withstand floods
and bushfires
and drought.

These pioneer plants
sprout first
after a landslide or fire.
Their seedlings enrich the soil with nitrogen
and bring the land back to life.

When flowering,
yellow ball-shaped blossoms
against bright green foliage
display Australia's national colors.

A symbol of resilience,
renewal,
and optimism
in an ancient land,
they're celebrated
each September first on Wattle Day.

Baobab

(Adansonia digitata)

National Tree of Angola, the Central African Republic, and Côte d'Ivoire

Baobabs loom over the landscape, appearing as though they're upside-down with their roots branching toward the sky.

Bulbous, pulpy trunks swell after rain and shrink during drought.

Called the Tree of Life, the baobab provides nourishment and shelter for animals and humans.

One immense hollowed trunk was transformed into a prison, another into a post office.

Baboons and elephants feast on their velvety fruit and disperse the seeds in their droppings—perfectly fertilized packages, ready to sprout.

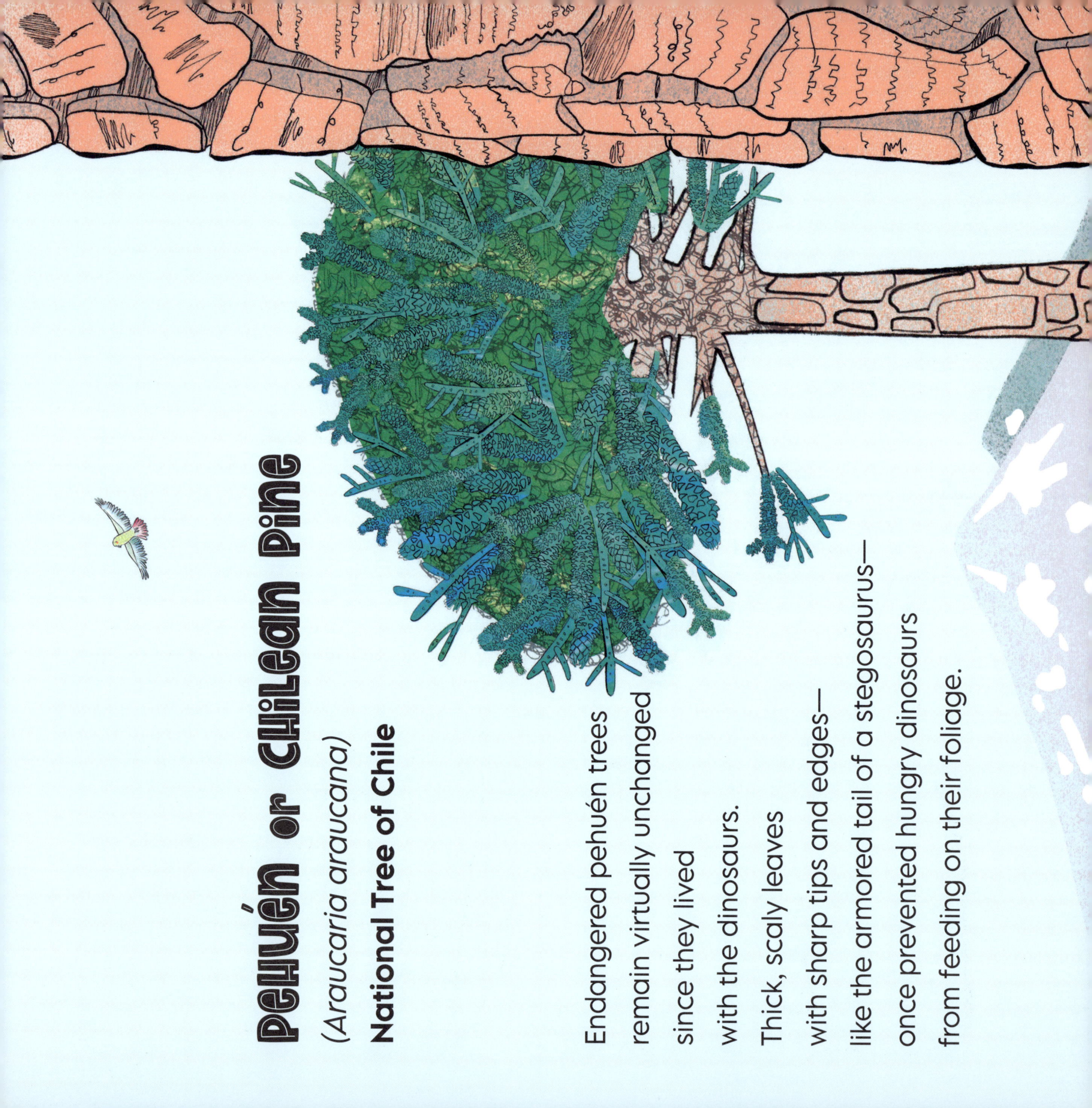

Pehuén or Chilean Pine

(*Araucaria araucana*)
National Tree of Chile

Endangered pehuén trees
remain virtually unchanged
since they lived
with the dinosaurs.
Thick, scaly leaves
with sharp tips and edges—
like the armored tail of a stegosaurus—
once prevented hungry dinosaurs
from feeding on their foliage.

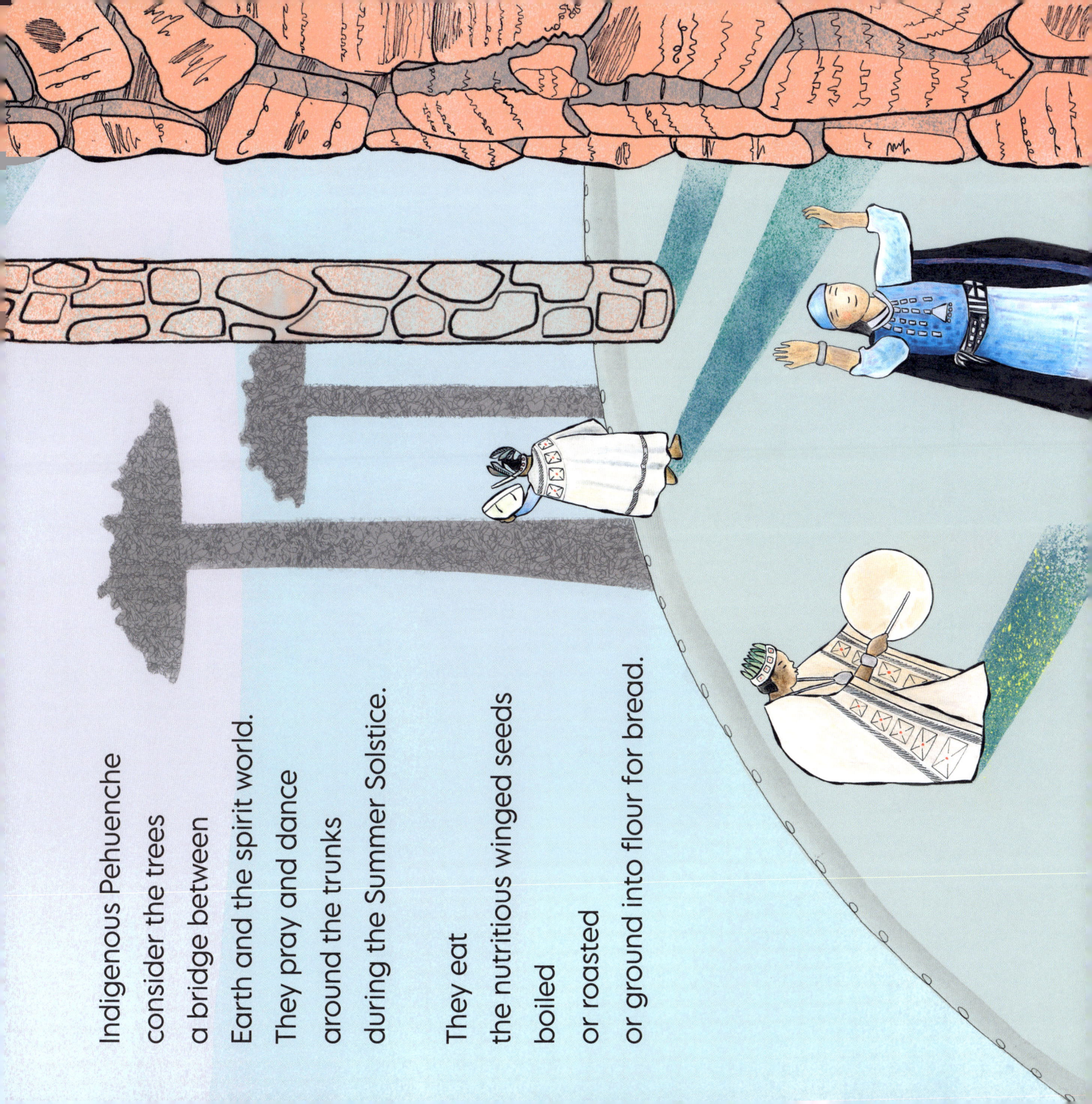

Indigenous Pehuenche
consider the trees
a bridge between
Earth and the spirit world.
They pray and dance
around the trunks
during the Summer Solstice.

They eat
the nutritious winged seeds
boiled
or roasted
or ground into flour for bread.

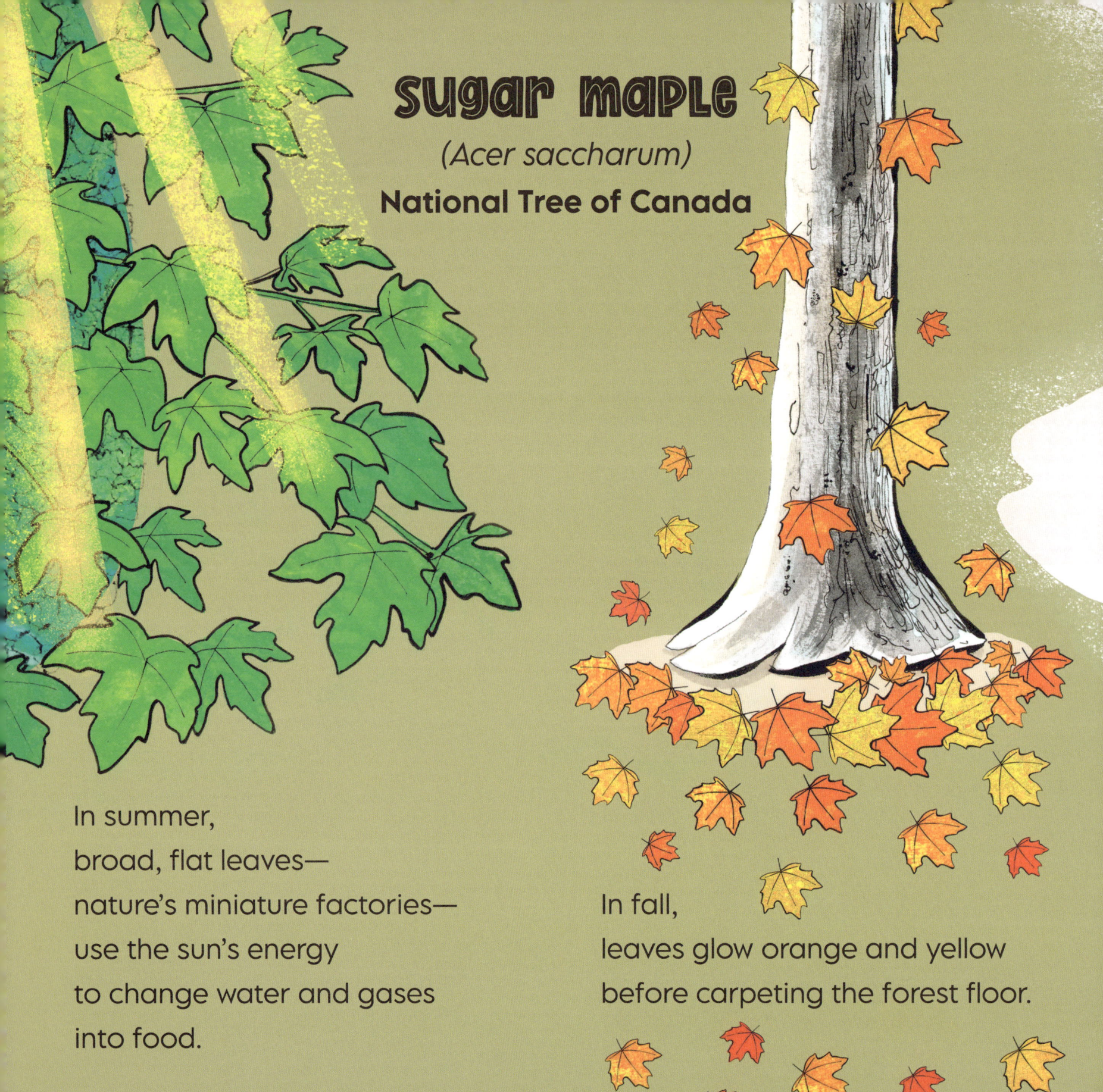

sugar maple
(Acer saccharum)
National Tree of Canada

In summer,
broad, flat leaves—
nature's miniature factories—
use the sun's energy
to change water and gases
into food.

In fall,
leaves glow orange and yellow
before carpeting the forest floor.

The tree rests in winter.

In spring,
energy stored
in the roots during winter
rushes
toward the crown as sugary sap.

When tapped,
sap slips
through a spout
into buckets or tubes
to be simmered into sweet
pancake-smothering syrup.

Quina or Fever Tree
(Cinchona officinalis)
National Tree of Peru and Ecuador

Deep in the Andean rainforest
a healing tree
hides among lush foliage.
Thin, with shiny green leaves,
its bark changed the course of history.

Indigenous people
who use the quina for medicine
once shared their knowledge
with Europeans who colonized their land.

For three hundred years,
quinine from its bitter bark
was the only cure
for the deadly fever-inducing disease
called malaria.

oak
(Quercus)

National Tree of the United States, England, and Ireland

Symbols of strength and endurance, long-lived oaks provide homes to hundreds of organisms. Woodpeckers hunting grubs drum holes in their trunks. Squirrels and blackbirds nest in their branches.

Humans use the wood to build houses and boats
   and cathedrals.

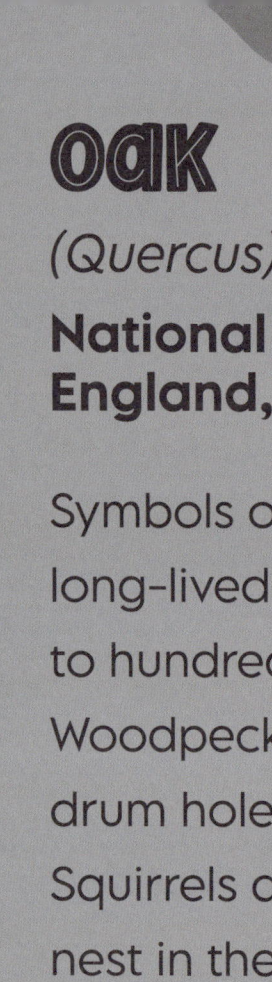

Tasty truffles, prized for woodsy flavors,
thrive among their roots.
The acorns feed pigs and sheep,
chipmunks and humans.

Oak is the tree
most frequently
struck by lightning.
The ancient Greeks
declared it the tree of Zeus,
hurler of thunderbolts.

Real Yellowwood
(Podocarpus latifolius)
National Tree of South Africa

These ancient trees
grow in mountainous forests
and along rocky hillsides.
In damp locations,
silvery gray lichen
called old man's beard
           hangs
                from their limbs.

The honey-colored wood
was favored for flooring and ceilings
in old homesteads.
It was prized for railroad ties
and butcher's blocks
and cupboards.

It provided a final resting place
when made into coffins.

Nearly lumbered to extinction,
real yellowwoods are now protected.

Narra or Rosewood Tree
(Pterocarpus indicus)

National Tree of the Philippines

The Narra thrives
in mountains and lowlands,
beside rocky shores and tidal creeks.

Its resilience and strength
symbolize the Filipinos' endurance
and struggle for independence.

The dome-shaped crown
flares with vibrant yellow flowers
for only one day.
Come morning,
the blossoms blanket the earth.

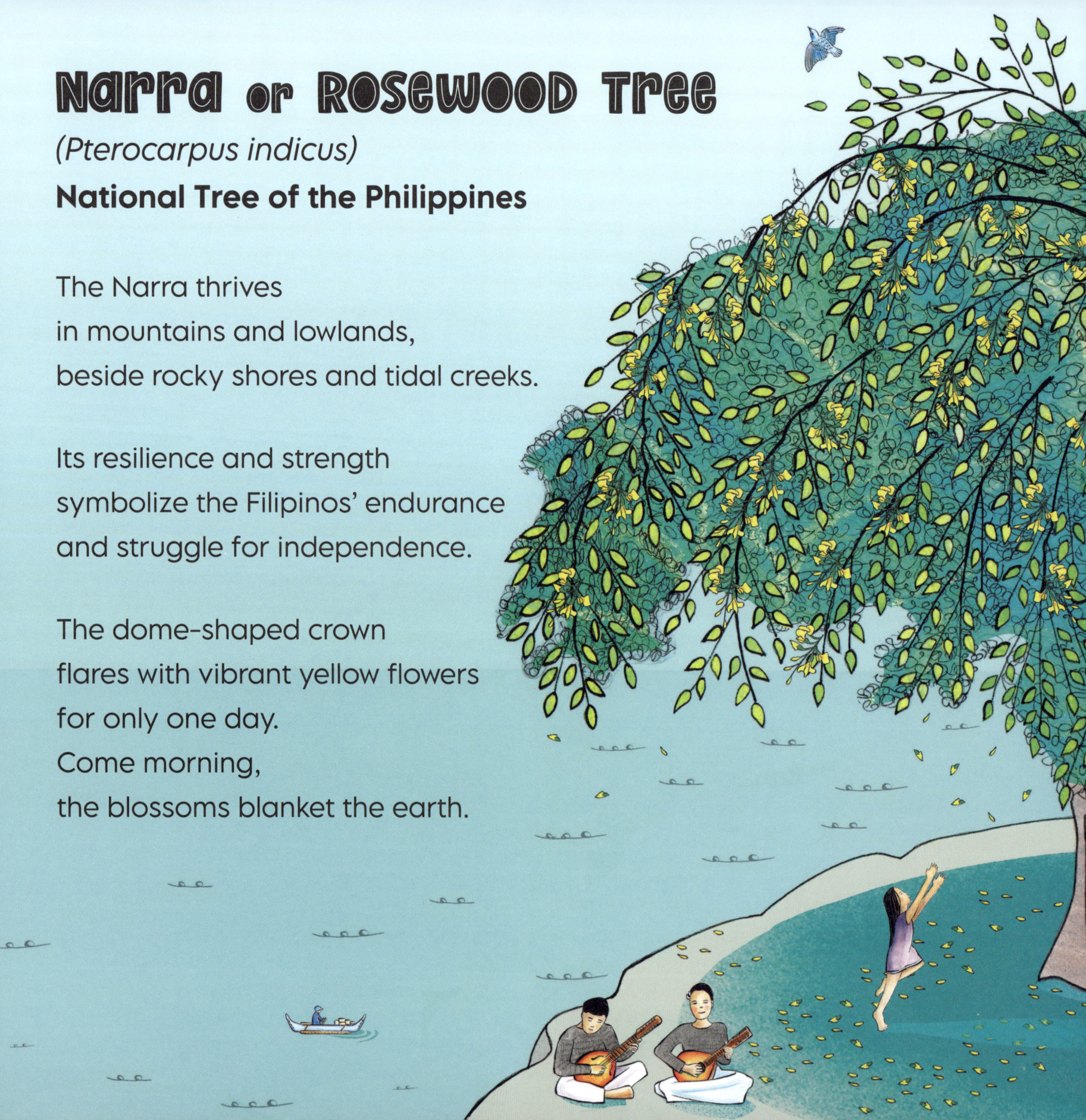

Soon, seed pods
shaped like flying saucers
dot the tree.
When they drop
they're carried away
by wind or water.

Its rose-scented wood—
resistant to termites and salt water—
is preferred for cabinets and furniture,
boats and musical instruments.

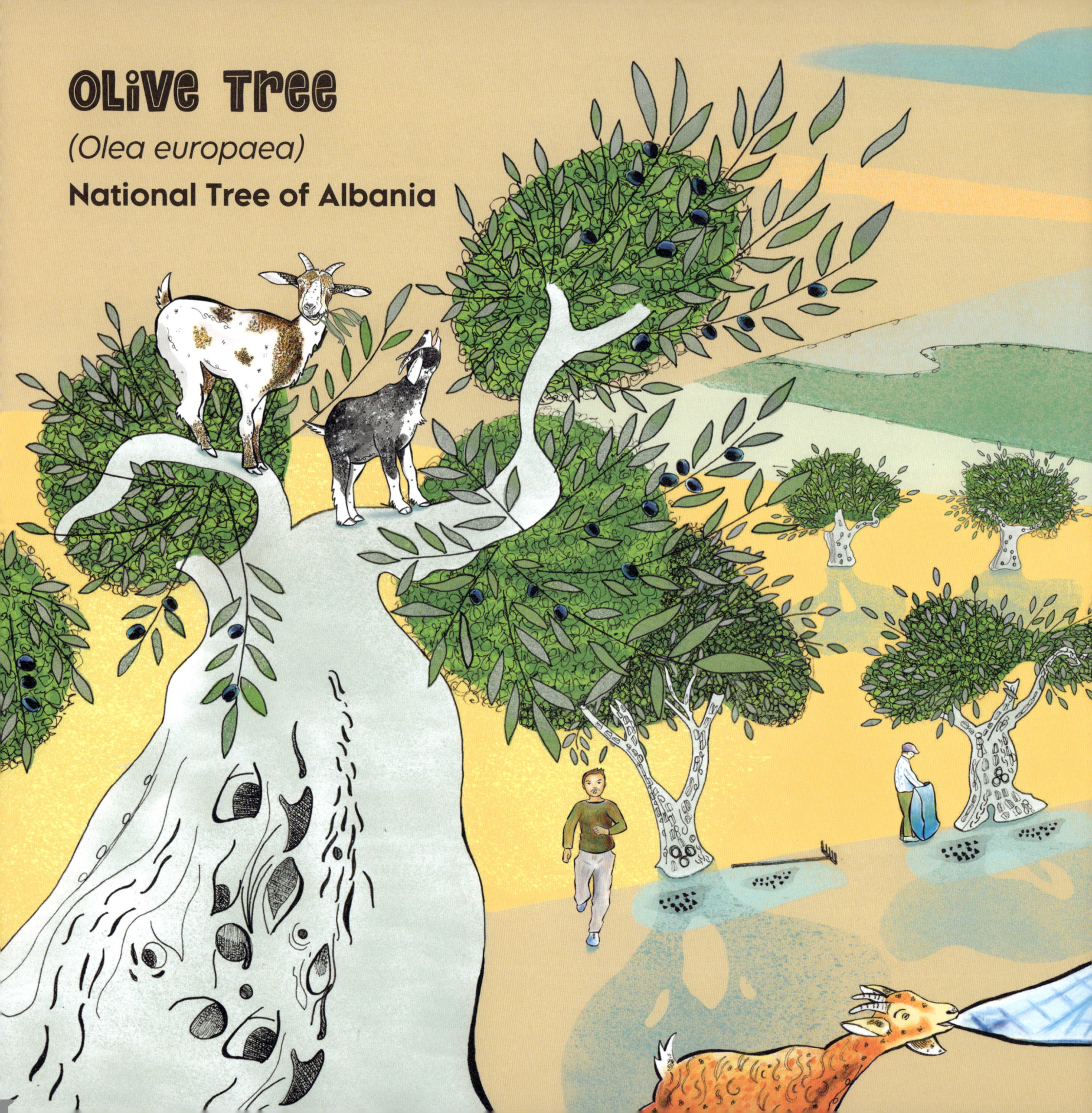

These sun-loving trees
tolerate heat
and drought
and hungry goats.

Squat, gnarled trunks
support puffballs
of dark, green-gray leaves
that shimmer and flash silver
in the breeze
like Flamenco dancers
flourishing their skirts.

Small, fragrant white flowers,
pollinated in spring,
ripen into shiny black olives
that release liquid gold
when pressed—
oil used for fuel,
lotions, and cooking—
valued for its health benefits
for more than six thousand years.

CUBAN ROYAL PALM
(Roystonea regia)

National Tree of Cuba

Tough, leathery leaves called fronds
are pointed at the tip
so water
        drips
        off
during tropical storms.
If winds blow
too strong,
fronds drop
to the ground
to prevent the tree
from toppling.

Hanging sprays
of heavily scented blooms
release a snowstorm of pollen.
Later, birds and bats feast
on fruit growing
           beneath
the feathery fronds.
Farmers fatten hogs
on the fruit.

Royal palms are woven
into the ceremonial practices
of Santería and Christianity,
the most popular
religions in Cuba.

Ginkgo
(Ginkgo biloba)

National Tree of China

These sacred trees
with fan-shaped leaves
once thrived across the planet
and survived the asteroid
that killed the dinosaurs.

Over time, ginkgoes dwindled
until they remained
in only a few places in China.

Traveling Buddhist monks
carried seeds
to temples and shrines
in Korea and Japan.

Several ginkgoes survived
the bombing of Hiroshima.
They sent out new shoots,
bringing comfort and hope
to the people.

Today, the offspring of those trees—
planted as symbols of peace—
thrive around the globe.

Trees feed us
calm us
    clothe us
        and cure us.
They purify the air
and provide oxygen we breathe.

Trees inspire
    myths and legends,
        arts and crafts.
They provide supplies
    for boats and bridges,
        tools and toys.
We make medicine from their bark
and books from their wood.
We rest in the shade
of their canopies
    and play in the ladder
        of their branches.

Our lives are intertwined with trees.
We honor
all that they give to the world
by planting new ones
for future generations.

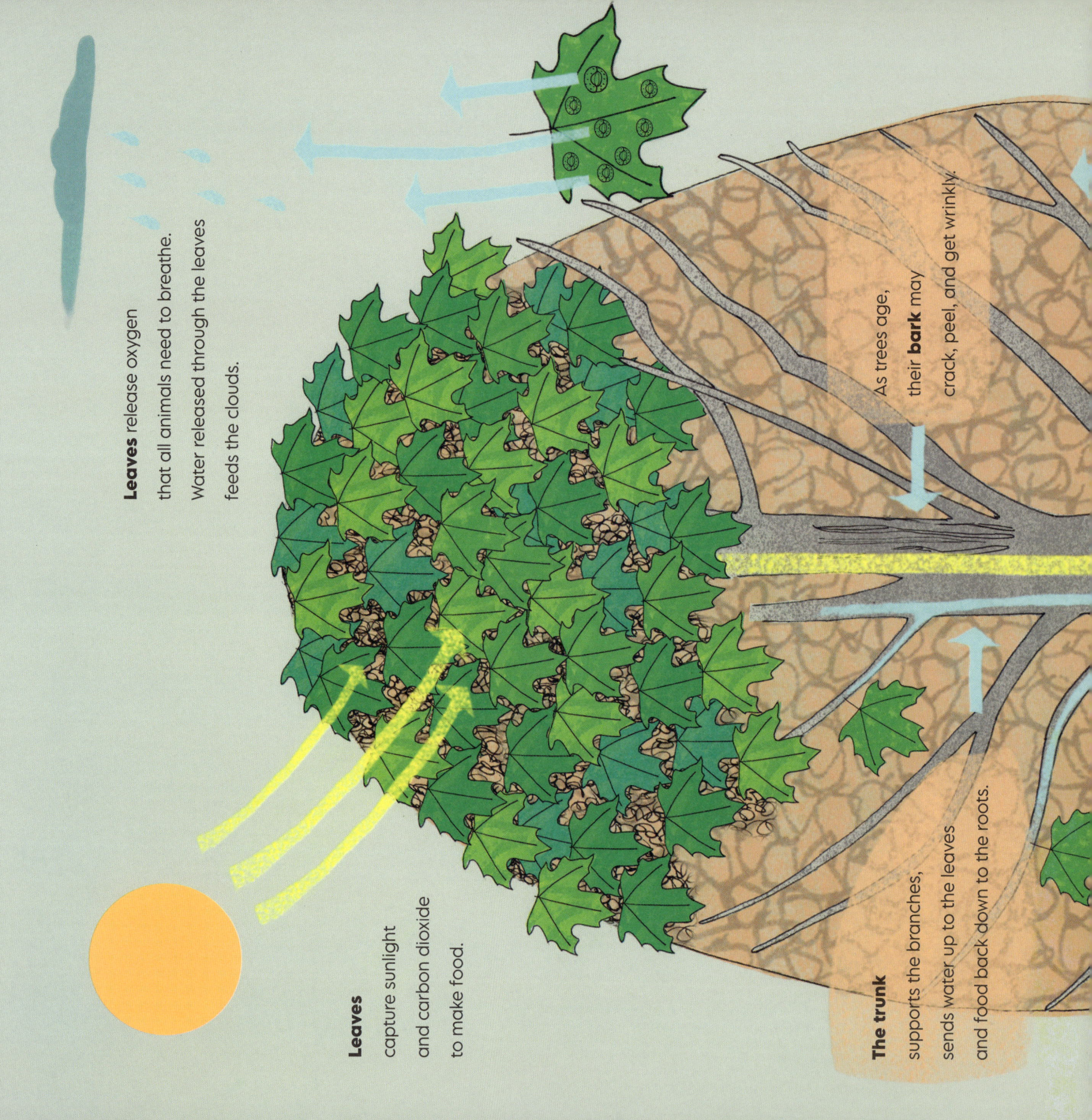

Leaves release oxygen that all animals need to breathe. Water released through the leaves feeds the clouds.

Leaves capture sunlight and carbon dioxide to make food.

As trees age, their **bark** may crack, peel, and get wrinkly.

The trunk supports the branches, sends water up to the leaves and food back down to the roots.

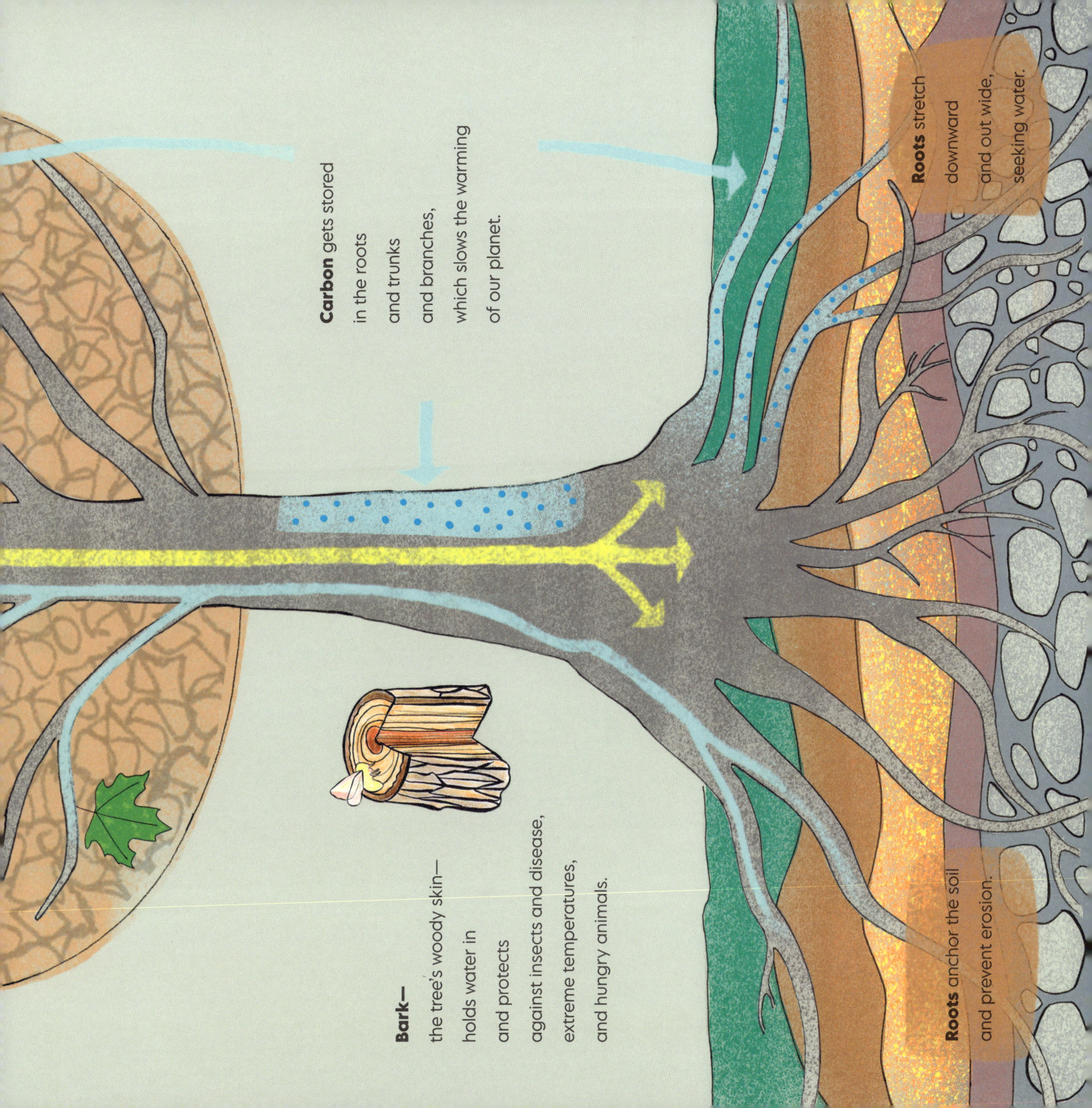

MORE FUN FACTS about the national trees you love (or will soon!)

✤ Can you spot the items listed below in the pages of the book?

BANYAN

The Banyan is one of the most sacred trees in Asia. It's considered the Tree of Knowledge and the Tree of Life. One tree in Kolkata (Calcutta) Botanical Gardens took about 200 years to become one of the world's largest trees. It has more than 1,775 prop roots and can shelter more than 20,000 people!

✤ **CAN YOU SPOT** the bold Indian Peafowl peeking out at you? That's the National Bird of India!

GOLDEN WATTLE

Wattle trees are named for "wattle and daub," a method English settlers in Australia used to build houses. Wattles (flexible sticks) created the framework and then were daubed with mud and dung to fill the cracks.

In the 1800s, settlers stripped the tree's bark to supply hundreds of leather-making tanneries with tannin. Soon tree seeds were sent around the world.

✤ **DID YOU KNOW** their edible seeds are gluten-free and high in protein?

BAOBAB

Set in Angola's Kissama National Park during the dry season, the baobab has dropped its leaves to conserve water, but the fruit stays on the tree until it dries out and falls to the ground. During the dry season, elephants gouge out parts of the trunk to get to its water and nutrients. This species of baobab lives all over Africa, but six species live only in Madagascar and one only in Australia.

✤ **CAN YOU SPOT** the zebras and giraffes?

Pehuén (pay when)

This page is set in Chile in the Conguillio National Park with a view of the Llaima Volcano. When pehuén are young, their shape resembles a Christmas tree, but as they grow, they drop the lower branches so they look like tall umbrellas. The bark also changes as the tree ages, becoming rough with irregular, deep ridges.

✢ **CAN YOU SPOT** the slender-billed parakeet? It isn't found anywhere else in the world and plays a key role in the tree's ecosystem.

Sugar Maple

In the late 1700s, maple sugar was the primary sweetener available in North America and was commonly used for bartering. Boiling the sap longer and at higher heat darkens the syrup's color and strengthens its flavor. Sugar maple seeds are called a maple key or double samara. Kids often toss them in the air to watch them whirl back down.

✢ **DID YOU KNOW** many maples were shipped to Japan to create bowling alleys in the 1970s?

Quina

Historians credit quinine as a key factor in the British Empire's expansion. Dutch and British colonists smuggled quina seeds to plantations in Asia. This enabled colonization to expand to areas where malaria was common. Historians say people speak English around the world partly because of quinine.

✢ **CAN YOU SPOT** a gray-breasted mountain toucan, a jaguar, a cock-of-the rock (Peru's national bird) and an Anopheles mosquito?

Oak

Oak trees have played a significant role in history. Queen Elizabeth I was reportedly sitting under an English oak when she learned she had become queen.

The Emancipation Oak at Hampton University in Virginia, USA provided shade for classes for African Americans who fled enslavement during the US Civil War. In January 1863, one of the first official public readings of the Emancipation Proclamation happened beneath the tree.

✚ **DID YOU KNOW** oaks can live more than 1,000 years?

Real Yellowwood

The lichen that hangs from these trees is not one organism. It's two organisms living together as one (usually, a fungus and algae). Real yellowwoods have provided more timber than any other indigenous tree in South Africa, which is why it's now protected. The foliage is covered in a bluish-gray powder that rubs off to expose green below.

✚ **CAN YOU SPOT** the Knysna turaco bird (or, in South Africa, the Knysna loerie) and Rameron pigeon?

Narra

The narra holds a special place in the hearts of Filipinos because it's intertwined with traditions, art, and the fight for freedom. The tree's strength and long life symbolize the strength and resilience of Filipinos, while its ability to thrive in varied conditions reflects the Filipinos' adaptability and endurance through many challenges, such as their fight for independence from colonizers.

✚ **CAN YOU SPOT** a whale fluke (tail) and an olive ridley turtle?

CUBAN ROYAL PALM

In the illustration, tropical storm winds are so strong that two fronds are falling to the ground and fruit is being blown everywhere! A Cuban Panama hat flies into the air and a line of white butterfly ginger lilies (Cuba's National Flower) follows it.

Hog enclosures often include royal palms so that the hogs can feed on the fruits as they drop to the ground.

✚ **CAN YOU SPOT** four Cuban parakeets huddled in the palms and two Cuban Trogons (Cuba's national bird)?

OLIVE

In the Albanian olive grove shown, people start work at dawn before the sun gets too hot. They use rakes—a traditional method—to harvest olives.

Olives are also important in places like Morocco, Greece, Italy, Palestine, Spain, Israel, and Portugal. Olive oil is significant in various religions and is a key element of Mediterranean diets. Olive branches are universally recognized as a symbol of peace.

✚ **CAN YOU SPOT** the hungry goats trying to eat the farmer's breakfast?

GINKGO

Ginkgoes are sacred in East Asia and are often planted near Taoist and Buddhist temples. They're also planted along city streets around the world because they're resilient. However, planners do their best to avoid planting female trees because they produce stinky seeds (the outer fleshy part smells like vomit). Individual branches on some trees have been documented changing their sex from male to female.

✚ **CAN YOU SPOT** sparrows and a red-crowned crane—China's national bird?

Author's Note
Michelle Cusolito

Trees have played an important role in my life. My home is surrounded by a forest, where I often spend time among the majestic beeches, oaks, and white pines. I've hugged many trees around the world, including a baobab in Niger, olives in Morocco, and many ginkgoes and maples near my home. I'm especially happy to include the Narra because I lived in the Philippines as a teen and that country holds a special place in my heart. Even when I've lived in cities, I've always found trees to sit beneath.

www.michellecusolito.com | @mcusolito

Illustrator's Note
Marya Wright

All artists love trees! They inspire us to make art that connects us to nature. I wanted to create a book that celebrates national trees around the world and their importance to different cultures. I wanted to show how these trees live in their landscapes, alongside all the many animals and us humans. Trees are always there, looking over us, changing through the seasons, bringing us feelings of awe, wonder, and peace. Trees are magnificent and magical, and—like Michelle—I love to hug them!

@maryawrightillustrates

Learn more

✤ BOOKS
- Gianferrari, Maria. *Be a Tree!* Harry N. Abrams, 2021.
- Johnson, Jen Cullerton. *Seeds of Change.* Lee and Low Books, 2010.
- Judge, Lita. *The Wisdom of Trees: How Trees Work Together to Form a Natural Kingdom.* Roaring Brook Press, 2021.
- Kulekjian, Jessica. *Before We Stood Tall: From Small Seed to Mighty Tree.* Kids Can Press. Toronto, 2021.
- Messner, Kate. *Over and Under the Rain Forest.* Chronicle, 2020.
- Johnston, Tony & Bozic, Tiffany. *Trees.* Simon & Schuster/Paula Wiseman Books, 2021.

✤ WEBSITES
- Field guide to trees with tips for getting to know trees in your neighborhood. kids.nationalgeographic.com/books/article/field-guide-trees/
- Youth Education: Everything you need to inspire the next generation of tree planters in your classroom. arborday.org/kids/
- Make the forest part of your family's story. Find a forest or park near you to get started. discovertheforest.org/
- One Tree Planted: Planting trees across six global regions in over eighty countries. onetreeplanted.org/
- Plant for the Planet: Young People Fight the Climate Crisis. plant-for-the-planet.org/
- Wangari Maathai Foundation: Discover how Wangari's legacy lives on around the globe. wangarimaathai.org/

✤ SOURCES

Researching for this book presented a unique challenge because the trees featured grow on six different continents. We consulted dozens and dozens of sources over the course of a year. Sometimes, one government website would list the official tree, but we'd need to consult many others to learn details about the tree and its connections to people. Listing all of our sources would be impossible. These were some of the most helpful.

Websites
- The Royal Botanic Gardens at Kew kew.org/
- The US Herbarium collections.nmnh.si.edu/search/botany/
- Palmweb: Palms of the World Online palmweb.org/
- The Tree That Changed the World Map bbc.co.uk/travel/article/20200527-the-tree-that-changed-the-world-map/
- The Gymnosperm Database conifers.org/
- National Tropical Botanical Garden ntbg.org/
- The Baobab Foundation baobabfoundation.co.za/
- Botanic Gardens of Sydney botanicgardens.org.au/
- The Australian Virtual Herbarium avh.chah.org.au/

Books
- Carey, Francis. *The Tree: Meaning and Myth.* British Museum, 2012.
- Hagender, Fred. *The Meaning of Trees: Botany, History, Healing, Lore.* Chronicle Books, 2005.
- Hora, Bayard. *Oxford Encyclopedia of Trees of the World.* Crescent Books, 1986.
- Minahan, James. *The Complete Guide to National Symbols and Emblems, vol 1 and 2.* Greenwood Press, 2010.
- Oseid, Kelsey. *Trees: An Illustrated Guide.* Ten Speed Press, 2023
- Rupp, Rebecca. *Red Oaks and Black Birches: The Science and Lore of Trees.* Garden Way, 1992.
- Sibley, David Allen. *The Sibley Guide to Trees.* Knopf, 2009.
- van der Schans, Anton. *Tropical and Subtropical Trees: An Encyclopedia.* Timber Press, 2004.

Podcast
- *Completely Arbortrary* with Alex K. Crowson and J. Casey Clapp. arbortrarypod.com/

✤ ACKNOWLEDGMENTS

With special thanks to John Berryhill, Director of the Botanic Garden of Smith College, and Kady Wilson, Manager of Living Collections at the Botanic Garden of Smith College, for reviewing the text and illustrations for accuracy. Any mistakes that remain are our own.

Finally, thank you to James McGowan and the Moon + Bird publishing team of Fiona Robertson, Laura Whitaker-Jones, Karen Smith, Brittany Willis, Hayley Moss, Christiana Spens, and Gigi St John, for bringing *Rooted In Wonder* to life.

ROOTED IN WONDER

Michelle Cusolito

Illustrated by Marya Wright

First published in the UK and USA in 2026
by Moon + Bird, an imprint of Watkins Media Limited
Unit 11, Shepperton House, 83–89 Shepperton Road, London N1 3DF

info@moonandbirdbooks.com

Design and Typography copyright © Watkins Media Limited 2026
Text copyright © Michelle Cusolito 2026
Illustration copyright © Marya Wright 2026

The right of Michelle Cusolito to be identified as the Author of this text has been asserted in accordance with the Copyright, Designs and Patents Act of 1988. All rights reserved. No part of this book may be reproduced in any form or by any electronic or mechanical means, including information storage and retrieval systems, without permission in writing from the publisher, except by a reviewer who may quote brief passages in a review.

Publisher: Laura Whitaker-Jones
Commissioning Editor: Fiona Robertson
Copy Editor: Georgina Brown
Head of Design: Karen Smith
Production: Uzma Taj

A CIP record for this book is available from the British Library

ISBN: 978-1-78678-963-1 (Hardback)
ISBN: 978-1-91719-430-3 (eBook)

The manufacturer's authorised representative in the EU for product safety is:
eucomply OÜ - Pärnu mnt 139b-14, 11317 Tallinn, Estonia,
hello@eucompliancepartner.com, www.eucompliancepartner.com

10 9 8 7 6 5 4 3 2 1

Printed in China

www.moonandbirdbooks.com

"The lasting pleasures of contact with the natural world are not reserved for scientists but are available to anyone who will place themself under the influence of earth, sea, and sky and their amazing life."

Rachel Carson,
The Sense of Wonder: A Celebration of Nature for Parents and Children